YOUR KNOWLEDGE HAS VALUE

Companies Under Crisis. How to Motivate Employees Whilst Facing Restructuring?

Felix-Sebastian Ament

Bibliographic information published by the German National Library:

The German National Library lists this publication in the National Bibliography; detailed bibliographic data are available on the Internet at http://dnb.dnb.de.

ISBN: 9783346235787
This book is also available as an ebook.

© GRIN Publishing GmbH
Nymphenburger Straße 86
80636 München

Print and binding: Books on Demand GmbH, Norderstedt, Germany
Printed on acid-free paper from responsible sources.

The present work has been carefully prepared. Nevertheless, authors and publishers do not incur liability for the correctness of information, notes, links and advice as well as any printing errors.

GRIN web shop: https://www.grin.com/document/916289

Assignment – HR & Leadership Competencies

Felix-S. Ament

Companies under crisis – the impact of employee motivation

How employees can be motived while a mid-size company is facing restructuring

FOM Hochschule für Oekonomie & Management

Table of contents

List of abbreviations

Cum.	Cumulated
Dec.	December
KPI	Key Performance Indicator
Nov.	November
Thous.	Thousand
€	Euro

List of figures

1 Introduction

In 2018, 19,552 companies filed for insolvency in Germany. [1] Reasons for this can be found in the lack of objectives in controlling and in the effects of poor management styles during restructuring.[2]

This figure can also often be attributed to the alternating relationship between corporate crises and employees. Destructive feelings arising from the crisis, such as anxiety and stress perception of the employees, result in a lack of motivation, which further accelerates the crisis process by reducing the productivity of a company.[3]

Against this background, it is important to find ways to motivate employees during a restructuring process in order to ensure that it achieves its objective of protecting the company from insolvency

---

[1] (CRIF Bürgel GmbH, 2019)
[2] Calculated based on (Obmann, 2019)
[3] Ct. (Obmann, 2019) (KRAUS GHENDLER RUVINSKIJ Anwaltskanzlei, 2019)

2 Research questions and reflection

2.1   The aim of the work

The objective of the study is to understand the motivation of employees in the context of a company crisis.

The paper aims to give the reader a theoretical insight into the phases of a company crisis and then to show the resulting effects on employees. Building on this, a method for motivating employees is presented, which is then applied in practice in a concrete example of a medium-sized company. The application of the method is only explained and illustrated in the course of the practical context. The aim of the work should not be to demonstrate the effectiveness of the method itself. Rather, the aim is to investigate the significance and implementation of employee motivation method in connection with a successful restructuring method.

At the end of this paper, the reader will be shown the practical application of the used method of employee motivation in a company restructuring. This should finally answer the question of how employees can be motived when a mid-size company is facing re-structuring.

2.2 The current state of research

The graduate psychologist Prof. Dr. Florian Becker summarizes the state of research employee motivation in his book. He describes the increasing relevance of employee motivation in an entrepreneurial context. Research data also shows clear correlations between employee motivation and a company culture of high performance, innovation, customer satisfaction, and productivity. Prof. Dr. Becker sees a problem in the stigmatic application of motivational theories. From today's perspective, representatives of these theories, such as Maslow's pyramid of needs[4], offer only limited practical benefits. A naive application of content theories often leads to wrong assumptions.[5]

Similarly, Jürgen W. Goldfuß deviates from the pure application of motivation theories. In his book, he addresses the determinants of openness, credibility, and truthfulness. Jürgen W. Goldfuß explains how to steer your employees authentically and credibly through upcoming changes caused by crises.[6]

Lars Kuring also takes this view. In his article "Employee Leadership in the Crisis" he provides readers with research data, conducted as part of an online panel survey of 500 employees. The sample was distributed across Germany throughout all industries in November 2009.[7] The survey shows that 35% of employees feel left alone with their worries and fears during a crisis, due to inadequate information policy lacking the "openness" advocated by Jürgen W. Goldfuß. Furthermore, Lars Kuring emphasizes the importance of transparent objectives, which positively influence the motivation of the employees.[8] Prof. Dr. Florian Becker shows similar positive effects in his research. According to him, optimized goals lead to the optimization of the desired behavior. With the right formulation of goals, the motivation of employees can be significantly increased. One motivation theory that makes use of these principles is the "Goal Setting Theory after Locke and Gary Latham".[9]

---

[4] (Landeszentrale für politische Bildung, 2017)
[5] Ct. (Prof. Dr. Becker, 2019, p. 217 ff.)
[6] Ct. (Goldfuß, 2015, p. 1 ff.) (Springer Nature Switzerland AG, 2015)
[7] Ct. (Kuring, 2010)
[8] Ct. (Kuring, 2010)
[9] Ct. (Prof. Dr. Becker, 2019, p. 117 ff.)

2.3 Structure and methodology

This paper is divided into five chapters. The introduction is followed by an outline of the purpose of the work, the current state of research and the methodology. Chapter three then provides the theoretical basis for practical chapter four. The final part of the paper, chapter five, serves to present the findings of the investigations.

In order to find out how employees in medium-sized companies can be motivated during restructuring, a qualitative study was carried out. For this purpose, relevant technical literature was analyzed within the framework of a literature search and used as a basis for implementation in the sample company.

In order to identify suitable motivation models for company structuring, Google Scholar was used to searching for specialist literature from experts in the restructuring environment and human resources. The intersections of the literature identified were then summarized. Newspaper articles, in which the current situation in relation to this topic is described more exactly, were likewise included in the investigation.

The data and information gained from the research were combined with the selected motivation model "Goal-Setting-Theory after Locke and Gary Latham" in practical application in the company.

3 Companies and employees in times of difficulties

3.1   Phases of corporate crises

The course of a corporate crisis can be depicted using Reiner Müller's four-phase model, which is shown in Figure 1 below.

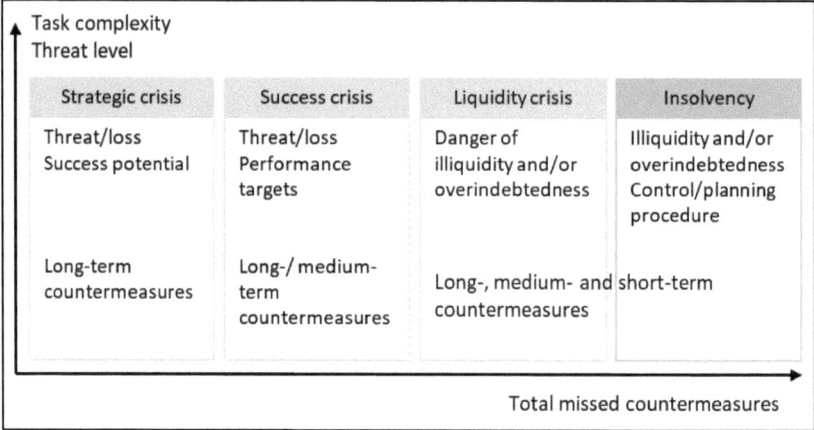

Figure 1: Development of the corporate crisis[10]

The starting point is the strategic crisis, in which the long-term success potential of the company is threatened. This can include an image-rich product or company brand. If the company's financial goals such as sales or results are not subsequently achieved, this is referred to as a succession crisis. In this crisis phase, the implementation of the key success targets is questioned. At this point, the company is already unprofitable and there is a risk of over-indebtedness. If there is still a failure to meet corporate targets, there is an acute risk of insolvency and talks of liquidity crisis begin. Now the legal crises caused by the threat of illiquidity and/or over-indebtedness are coming to the fore.[11]

In the case of corporations, the most common legal form in German SMEs[12], a company enters the insolvency phase as soon as it is overindebted.

---

[10] (Müller, 1982)
[11] (Prof. Dr. Hommel, et al., 2006, p. 34 f.)
[12] (Statistisches Bundesamt, 2019)

Over-indebtedness in insolvency is described in section 19 (2) InsO. "Over-indebtedness occurs when the debtor's assets no longer cover the existing liabilities unless the continuation of the company is predominantly probable under the circumstances".[13]

Within the framework of the Insolvency Ordinance, judicial reorganization is possible. The basis for the implementation is, among other things, a prepared restructuring concept. This concept contains standard measures that have a direct influence on the affected employees.[14]

---

[13] Translated and quoted by (§ 19 Abs. 2 InsO)
[14] Ct. (Prof. Dr. Hommel, et al., 2006, p. 34 f.) (Dr. Dr. Hohberger & Damlachi, 2010, p. 25)

3.2   Effects on employees

Once the restructuring concept has been approved, immediate measures are imple-
mented. The first step is to involve all the parties involved (suppliers, management,
banks, employees, etc.). This is followed by measures, which are difficult to enforce in
the HR department due to legal restrictions and the counteraction of individual employees.[15]

Typical company-wide measures with direct effects on employees include restructuring
the organization to tight processes, carrying out an overhead cost-value analysis, closing
or reducing unprofitable departments, and finally, dismissal or possible hiring of employees. In addition to salary cuts, personnel management measures also include
changes in management and authority to issue directives. Further measures include en-
forcing short-time working and ordering unpaid overtime. The employees of a company
are also exposed to errors and misconduct by their managers, instead of finding new
solutions, the management clings to earlier concepts. There is a lack of delegation, team
behavior and participation. Employees are not involved in decisions and yet management demands loyalty and support. The totality of measures in combination with wrong
management behavior accelerates the course of the crisis and leads to further escala-
tion. The motivation within the company decreases and the employees get scared. This
fear blocks motivation, creativity, and courage, which causes productivity to drop by up
to 50%.[16]

In order to avoid the typical leadership mistakes in crisis management, to reduce fear
and to increase motivation, the non-stigmatic inclusion of motivation models and employee participation is required.[17] The current state of research shows that although
motivation can be increased by formulating optimized goals, it should be complemented
by open, credible and truthful communication in the form of employee involvement.

---

[15] Ct. (Dr. Dr. Hohberger & Damlachi, 2010, p. 64)
[16] (Schüller, 2017)
[17] Ct. (Dr. Schlebusch, et al., 1999, pp. 452-456) (Dr. Dr. Hohberger & Damlachi, 2010, p. 64 ff.)

3.3   Goal-Setting-Theory after Locke and Gary Latham

In 1968 Edwin A. Locke published his theory of objectives in "Toward a Theory of Task Motivation and Incentive". He showed that employees are motivated by clear, well-defined goals and feedback. Locke found that goals formulated in KPIs are much more effective than vague instructions. He explained that the formulation of almost unattainable goals results in harder work, increased effectiveness, and increased creativity.[18]

In the 1990s, Dr. Gary Latham Locke examined the theory in practice and concluded that the link between goal setting and performance is both existential and essential. Following the research, Locke and Latham jointly published "A Theory of Goal Setting & Task Performance", which is an extension of the 1968 theory of goal setting.

Their theory also emphasizes the relevance of employee involvement to achieve a goal. This has been shown to further motivate. According to Locke, for employees to feel motivated to achieve a goal, they must be involved in the evaluation of objectives and allowed some room to maneuver in order to achieve said goal.

Edwin A. Locke and Dr. Gary Latham set out the following five principles of effective goal setting in the management manual:

1. Clarity. A goal must be clearly formulated.

2. Challenge. Unattainable goals lead to harder work, increased effectiveness and increased creativity.

3. Commitment. Employees must believe in the goal from the beginning.

4. Feedback. Regular measurement and reporting on the process.

5. The complexity of tasks. Realistic creation of schedules and splitting the process into stages.

In addition, it is important that employees have the required knowledge and skills when defining their goals.[19]

---

[18] Ct. (Locke , 1968)
[19] Ct. (Locke & Latham, 1991) (Young, 2017)

Chapters 2.2 and 3.2 show that the theories of Locke and Gary Latham can be applied appropriately in the case of restructuring. In addition, the theory also implies that aspects of employee participation, should also be used to motivate employees during a restructuring.[20]

---

[20] Ct. (Locke & Latham, 1991) (Young, 2017)

4 Implementation in the company

4.1 Project overview

The sample company has its headquarters in Ilsfeld, Germany. The business activity is the development, production, and distribution of protection systems against falls from heights for persons and loads. In 2019, the company employed around 100 people and generated sales of around EUR 15 million. The company has been undergoing bank-induced restructuring since May 2019, which is the final phase of a corporate crisis.

The sub-project of the restructuring is an order-to-cash process, which operationally affected the purchasing, production and logistics departments. The aim of the two-month process was to be able to book the maximum possible mount out of and an order backlog of around EUR 2 million. The sales target was EUR 1.5 million in November 2019 and EUR 1.7 million in December 2019. In order to achieve this, the 20 affected employees had to be motivated to achieve peak performance. Among other things, this involved working Saturdays and daily overtime.

This chapter describes how the target theory from chapter 3.3 is interwoven with the aspect of employee participation and made a significant contribution to achieving the sales targets.

4.2 Goal setting and employee participation

At the start of the project in November 2019, a joint meeting was held with the employees of concerned departments and management. In accordance with the principle of participation, the financial situation was first communicated by the management.[21] Subsequently, the sales targets for the next two months were presented, and measures were discussed. The employees were motivated to bring in their own suggestions that could contribute to achieving the goals. The suggestions were evaluated together and integrated into a mutually agreed catalog of measures.

In the next step, departmental targets were defined. For example, orders were prioritized in the order backlog and then missing parts lists were created. These lists were used as a joint working document by purchasing and production, whereby the main target was broken down into small targets at order level according to Locke and Gary Latham. The clear and unambiguous formulation of the objectives was the timely procurement of the missing parts and the determination of the exact production output at the parts level. In logistics, the number of "orders yet to be packed" was used as the only KPI.

The objectives in all departments were beyond the realm of possibility. Nevertheless, the purchasers were motivated and spurred on every day by daily follow-ups with the suppliers to shorten delivery times and arrange for partial deliveries.

In production, the target output was just over 20% of the average output of the past months of 2019, where personnel capacities were actively increased by auxiliary staff to justify the high target and to provide the necessary resources, according to Locke and Gary Latham. The logistics department was told to reduce the number of orders still to be packed to 0 every day, this had not been achieved in 2019 yet.

In order to keep the employees informed of the achievement of this goal and to motivate them further, a report was sent out every morning. This report was directed at the individual goals of the departments and at the same time put them into the context of the sales analysis.

---

[21] Ct. (Dombrowski & Quack, 2007)

This allowed the employees to see exactly how their performance affected the achievement of the overall goal. The results were discussed in 10-minute meetings twice a day, during these meetings, employees were encouraged to make suggestions for improvement on how to make the process more effective without long lead times.

4.3 Evaluation and interpretation

The formulation of clear, almost impossible to achieve goals in combination with daily encouragement during the presentations of the individual reports resulted in a strong increase in motivation. As can be seen in Figure 2, the sales target could not be achieved in the first month. Nevertheless, motivation in logistics resulted in a reduction in the number of orders still to be packed from 78 to 21, even though production steadily increased the pressure on logistics due to rising output.

In December 2019, the sales target was only just missed, as can be seen in Figure 3. This turnover could only be achieved through the hard work of all departments involved. Although the target was considered almost impossible at the beginning of November 2019, Figure 5 shows that logistics managed to reduce its KPI to 0. The joint meetings also made a significant contribution to sales. When difficulties arose, such as IT problems, the increased creativity of the employees led to new solutions.

The analysis of the company example shows how employees can further improve their performance by increasing motivation even in difficult situations. The reasons for this can be found in the application of the Goal-Setting-Theory after Locke and Gary Latham in combination with successful employee participation.

5 Summary and outlook

As the present study shows, it is possible to motivate employees during a company crisis and thus achieve increased productivity in the company. The Goal-Setting-Theory of Locke and Gary Latham offers an approach to this, which in combination with the use of employee participation shows a solution to the research question. The results of the present study are limited to certain company size, industries, departments, workforce and a time course, which in their entirety can nevertheless be regarded as a critique of the work.

In subsequent research, it is necessary to investigate whether the findings from the company example described above are consistent with new studies. In addition, an exact measurement of employee motivation over time should be carried out. This also provides a data basis for comparing the method with others.

In summary, it can be said that clear and difficult to achieve target KPIs with constant employee involvement can lead to short-term motivation boosts in the company. Thus, even during restructuring, companies can achieve their sales targets and avoid the threat of insolvency.

List of sources

CRIF Bürgel GmbH, 2019. *statista.com.* [Online]
Available at:
https://de.statista.com/statistik/daten/studie/75215/umfrage/unternehmensinsolven
zen-in-deutschland-seit-2000/
[Accessed 21 12 2019].

Dombrowski, U. & Quack, S., 2007. Erfolgreiche Restrukturierungsprojekte durch
Mitarbeiterpartizipation. *ZWF Zeitschrift für wirtschaftlichen Fabrikbetrieb.*

Dr. Dr. Hohberger, S. & Damlachi, H., 2010. *Sanierung im Mittelstand.* Marburg:
Tectum.

Dr. Schlebusch, D. W., Volz, N. & Huke, P., 1999. Unternehmenskrisen im Mittelstand -.
Die Bank - Zeitschrift für Bankpolitik und Bankpraxis, 7, pp. 452-456.

Goldfuß, J. W., 2015. *Führen in Krisen- und Umbruchzeiten.* Wiesbaden: Gabler Verlag.

KRAUS GHENDLER RUVINSKIJ Anwaltskanzlei, 2019. *anwalt-kg.de.* [Online]

Available at: https://anwalt-

kg.de/newsbeitrag/gesellschaftsrecht/gruendungsberatung/13-gruende-fuer-die-

insolvenz-von-unternehmen/

[Accessed 21 12 2019].

Kuring, L., 2010. *Mitarbeiterführung in der Krise.* [Online]

Available at: https://www.handelsblatt.com/unternehmen/management/arbeitsklima-

mitarbeiterfuehrung-in-der-krise/3384424.html?ticket=ST-24596772-

Jx1zhmpbJz0lmQ2FlguQ-ap1

[Accessed 09 12 2019].

Landeszentrale für politische Bildung, 2017. *lpb-bw.de.* [Online]

Available at: https://www.lpb-

bw.de/fileadmin/Abteilung_III/jugend/pdf/ws_beteiligung_dings/2017/ws6_17/maslo

wsche_beduerfnispyramide.pdf

[Accessed 09 12 2019].

Locke, E. A., 1968. *Toward a Theory of Task Motivation and Incentive.* Maryland:

Elsevier Inc.

Locke, E. A. & Latham, G. P., 1991. *A Theory of Goal Setting & Task Performance.*

Maryland: University of Maryland.

Müller, R., 1982. *Krisenmanagement der Unternehmung.* Frankfurt am Main:

Kohlhammer Verlag.

Obmann, C., 2019. *handelsblatt.com.* [Online]
Available at: https://www.handelsblatt.com/unternehmen/management/karriere-woran-firmenwandel-so-oft-scheitert-und-wie-es-besser-geht/24171894.html?ticket=ST-37723106-MLcI1CKXrlzfT4MReMMg-ap1
[Accessed 21 12 2019].

Prof. Dr. Becker, F., 2019. *Mitarbeiter wirksam motivieren.* Berlin: Springer-Verlag Berlin Heidelberg.

Prof. Dr. Becker, F., 2019. *wpgs.de.* [Online]
Available at: https://wpgs.de/fachtexte/motivation/ziele-und-motivation-mitarbeiter-mit-zielen-motivieren/
[Accessed 09 12 2019].

Prof. Dr. Hommel, U., Prof. Dr. Knecht, T. C. & Dr. Wohlenberg, H., 2006. *Handbuch Unternehmensrestrukturierung.* Wiesbaden: Dr. Th. Gabler.

Schüller, A. M., 2017. *creditreform-magazin.de.* [Online]
Available at: https://creditreform-magazin.de/mittelstandsbotschafter/hoechste-zeit-warum-die-angst-aus-den-unternehmen-verschwinden-muss/
[Accessed 14 12 2019].

Springer Nature Switzerland AG, 2015. *springer.com*. [Online]
Available at: https://www.springer.com/de/book/9783658052089#aboutBook
[Accessed 09 12 2019].

Springer Nature Switzerland AG, 2019. *springer.com*. [Online]
Available at: https://www.springer.com/de/book/9783658052089
[Accessed 23 12 2019].

Statistisches Bundesamt, 2019. *statista.com*. [Online]
Available at:
https://de.statista.com/statistik/daten/studie/237346/umfrage/unternehmen-in-
deutschland-nach-rechtsform-und-anzahl-der-beschaeftigten/
[Accessed 14 12 2019].

Young, J., 2017. *peakon.com*. [Online]
Available at: https://peakon.com/de/blog/future-work-de/edwin-locke-
zielsetzungstheorie/
[Accessed 20 12 2019].

Appendix

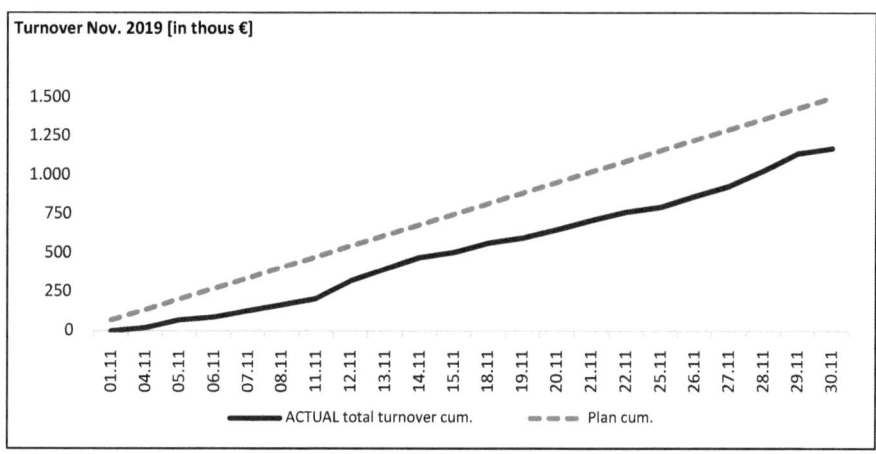

Figure 2: Sales measurement of the sample company on a daily basis Nov. 2019

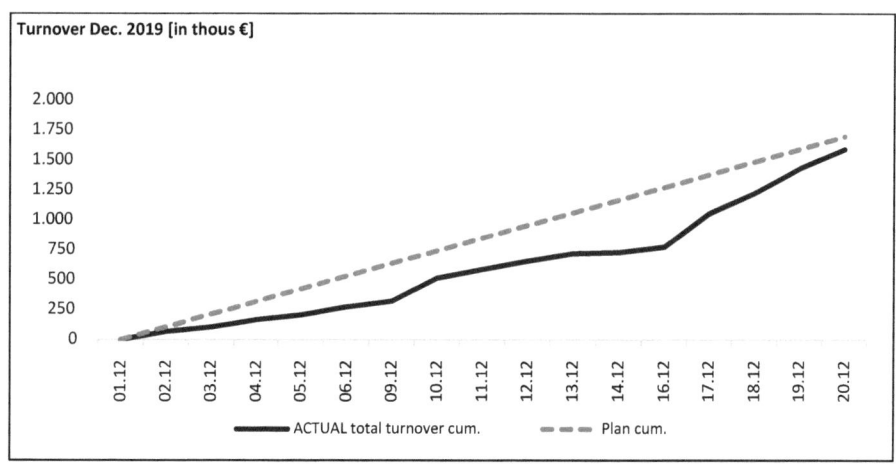

Figure 3: Sales measurement of the sample company on a daily basis Dec. 2019

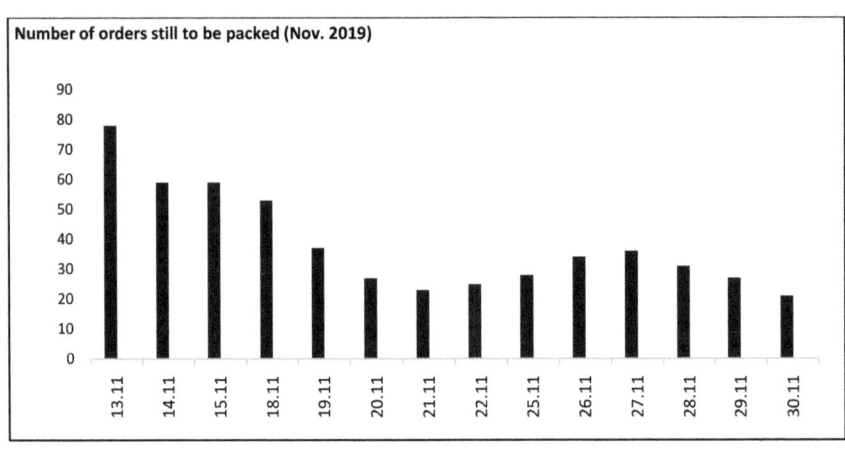

Figure 4: Daily measurement of the number of orders still to be packed of the example company Nov. 2019

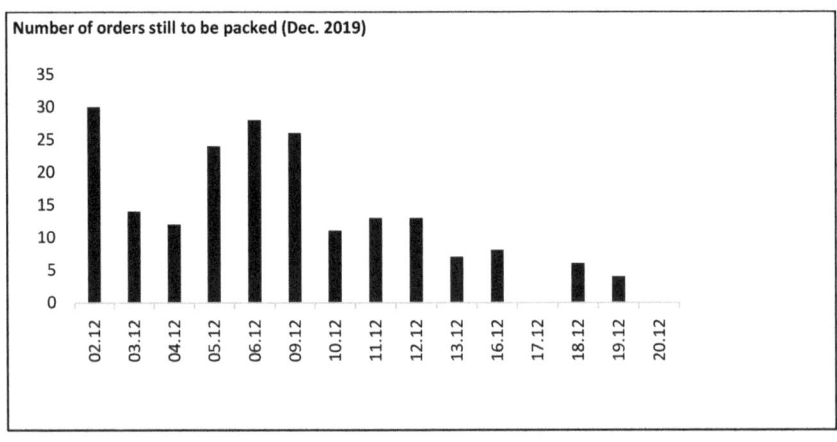

Figure 5: Daily measurement of the number of orders still to be packed of the example company Dec. 2019

YOUR KNOWLEDGE HAS VALUE